COUNTRY EXPLORERS

PUERTO RICO

JoAnn Milivojevic

Lerner Publications Company • Minneapolis

Lerner Publications Company
A division of Lerner Publishing Group, Inc.
241 First Avenue North
Minneapolis, MN 55401 U.S.A.

Website address: www.lernerbooks.com

Library of Congress Cataloging-in-Publication Data

Milivojevic, JoAnn.
    Puerto Rico / by JoAnn Milivojevic.
       p.   cm. — (Country explorers)
    Includes index.
    ISBN 978-1-58013-598-6 (lib. bdg. : alk. paper)
    1. Puerto Rico—Juvenile literature. 2. Puerto Rico—Geography—
Juvenile literature. I. Title.
    F1958.3.M563 2009
    972.95—dc22   2008008725

Manufactured in the United States of America
1 2 3 4 5 6 — PA — 14 13 12 11 10 09

Table of Contents

Welcome!

We're going to Puerto Rico! Puerto Rico is a U.S. commonwealth. A U.S. commonwealth is a territory that is owned by the United States.

Four islands make up the Commonwealth of Puerto Rico. The biggest island is called Puerto Rico. (No surprise there!) Two smaller islands rest off Puerto Rico's eastern coast. They're called Vieques and Culebra. Mona Island sits to the west. The Atlantic Ocean lies north of the four islands. To the south is the Caribbean Sea.

MONA ISLAND

Puerto Rico is made up of four islands, including Culebra *(right)*.

ATLANTIC
OCEAN

🌳	rain forest
▪	lowlands
⛰	mountains
◎	karst
★	country's capital

San Juan

PUERTO

RICO

CORDILLERA CENTRAL

Loíza

EL
YUNQUE

LUQUILLO
MOUNTAINS

SIERRA
DE CAYEY

CERRO
DE PUNTA

CULEBRINAS RIVER

ARECIBO RIVER

LA PLATA RIVER

Ponce

Guayama

CULEBRA

VIEQUES

CARIBBEAN
SEA

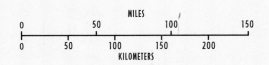

MILES				
0	50		100	150
0	50	100	150	200
		KILOMETERS		

Puerto
Rico

Beaches, Hills, and Mountains

Beaches and coves edge Puerto Rico's coasts. Sugarcane plants thrive in the eastern and western coastal valleys.

Puerto Rico has many beautiful beaches. This beach is near the capital city of San Juan.

Cone-shaped hills rise in the north. The hills are made of soft rock. Caves and craters lie among the hills. This landscape is called karst.

Mountains push up in the middle of the island. The Cordillera Central mountain range runs from east to west. The Luquillo Mountains stand in the northeast.

Winding rivers and roads mark the Cordillera Central mountain range.

Tropical Weather

Puerto Rico is a tropical country. Temperatures stay about 82°F (28°C) all year. Ocean breezes keep people cool. Sometimes storms called hurricanes strike the island. But Puerto Rico usually has mild weather.

Hurricane season can bring strong winds and rain to Puerto Rico.

Plants and flowers grow in a rain forest called El Yunque. Animals, birds, and lots of insects live there.

The Coquí

Puerto Rico's most famous rain forest creature is the *coquí (below)*. The coquí is a tiny frog. Its name comes from the sound it makes as night falls— "koh-KEE! koh-KEE!"

El Yunque lies in northeastern Puerto Rico. Many plants and animals thrive in El Yunque.

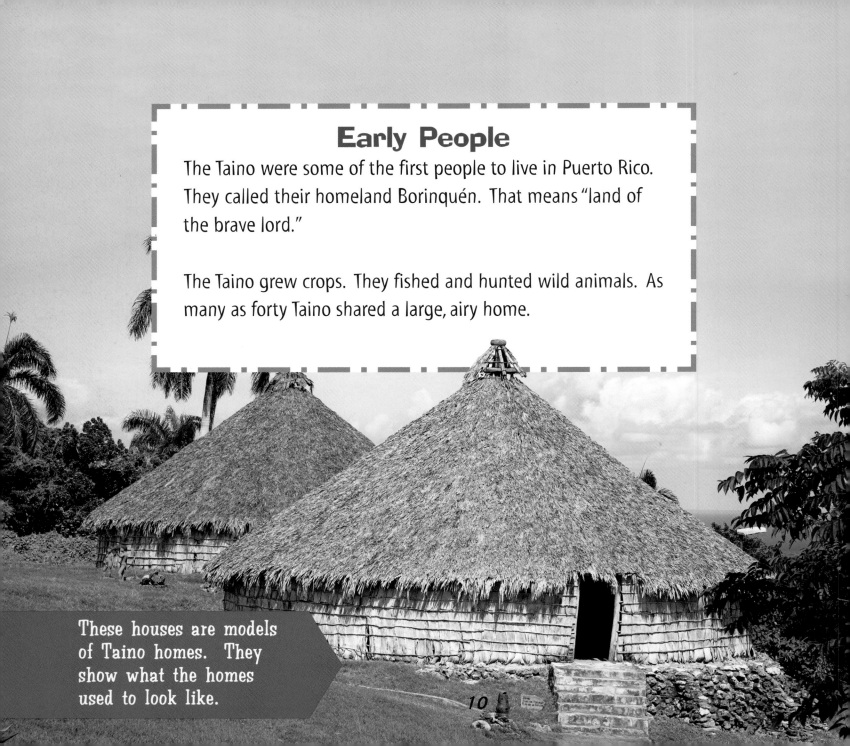

Early People

The Taino were some of the first people to live in Puerto Rico. They called their homeland Borinquén. That means "land of the brave lord."

The Taino grew crops. They fished and hunted wild animals. As many as forty Taino shared a large, airy home.

These houses are models of Taino homes. They show what the homes used to look like.

Taino artists carved wooden bowls and boxes. Weavers made clothing and low-hanging beds called hammocks. Taino traders paddled canoes to nearby islands to swap the handmade goods.

Taino artists made these stone carvings. The rocks are part of a park protected by the government.

Spanish Settlers

Christopher Columbus came to Borinquén in 1493. He claimed the land for Spain. Spanish settlers soon followed Columbus. They came in search of gold.

The settlers forced the Taino to work for them. They made the native people mine for gold. The settlers also spread diseases to the Taino. Many Taino died from these diseases.

This statue of Christopher Columbus stands in San Juan.

The settlers turned to farming when the gold ran low. They made the Taino work on large farms called plantations. The settlers also brought in slaves from Africa. They forced the slaves to work on the plantations too.

Name Switcheroo!

When Columbus arrived on Borinquén, he renamed the island San Juan Bautista. Spanish settlers named one of San Juan Bautista's towns Puerto Rico. (This means "rich port" in Spanish.) But in 1521, the town and the island switched names. The island became known as Puerto Rico. The town took on the name San Juan!

A worker picks coffee at a plantation in Puerto Rico. Early settlers made the Taino work at plantations such as this one.

Statues and buildings in the old part of San Juan date back to the time of Spanish settlement.

Changing Hands

Farming and trading grew when Spanish settlers were in charge. Cities began to spring up. But by the 1850s, the islanders wanted more freedom. Spain slowly started to give the islanders their independence.

By 1898, Puerto Rico had gained its freedom. Luis Muñoz Rivera became the first leader of the free country. But freedom didn't last long. The United States soon took over the island. In 1952, the island became a U.S. commonwealth.

Living in a Commonwealth

The people of the Puerto Rican commonwealth are U.S. citizens. They use U.S. money. They follow U.S. laws. They cannot vote for U.S. presidents. But they can make decisions about how to run their island.

A 1952 parade celebrates the creation of the Puerto Rican commonwealth.

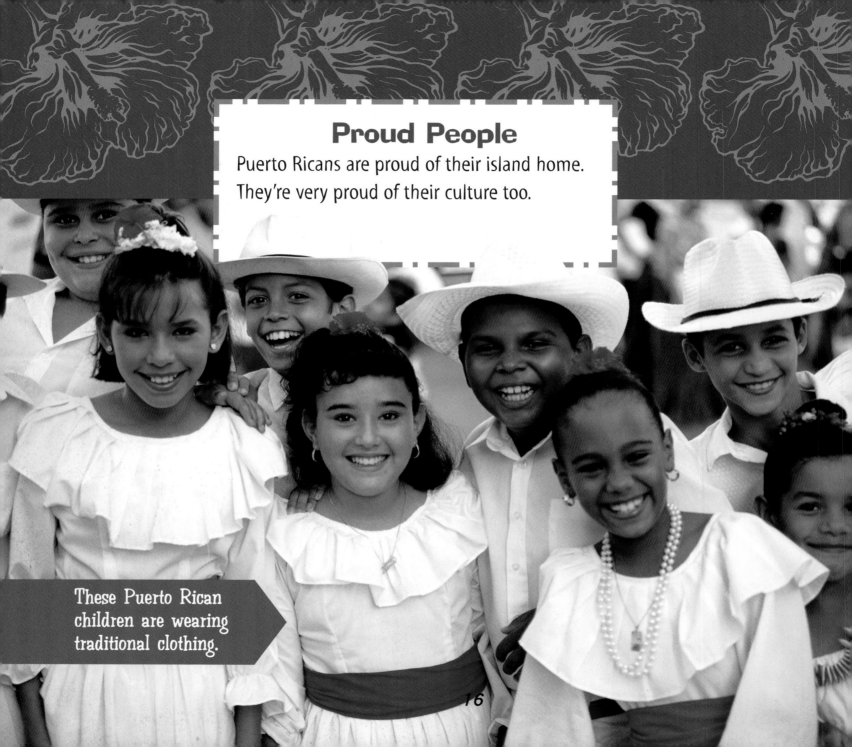

Proud People

Puerto Ricans are proud of their island home. They're very proud of their culture too.

These Puerto Rican children are wearing traditional clothing.

16

Some Puerto Ricans have Taino roots. Other islanders are African or Spanish. Still others are a mix of these three cultures.

Puerto Ricans come from different cultures—just like these teenagers skateboarding in San Juan.

City Slickers

Most Puerto Ricans live in cities. Puerto Rico's cities are busy places.

About 2 million people live in and around Puerto Rico's largest city, San Juan.

San Juan

San Juan is a bustling Puerto Rican city. The oldest part of San Juan is very beautiful. Visitors flock to this part of town. They like its cobblestone streets and historic houses. They also like exploring its interesting museums.

Life is modern for people in cities. Cars and buses whiz through the streets. Families talk on cell phones and use the Internet. Adults hurry off to work in high-rise buildings.

Old San Juan has cobblestone streets and brightly colored buildings.

Country Life

Life in the countryside moves more slowly. For fun, folks might gather to sing songs and play games. Village stores called *colmados* are common meeting spots. Neighbors meet at colmados to talk and share news.

People often meet at stores in Puerto Rican villages.

Fruit and vegetables are on display at this farmers' market in Puerto Rico.

People in the country might farm for a living. They grow food for the family and sell extra goods at markets. Puerto Rican farmers might grow sugarcane or pineapples.

Family Matters

In the countryside, some kids share a home with their parents, grandparents, aunts, and uncles. This arrangement is known as an extended family.

Both extended families and smaller families are close in Puerto Rico. Family members enjoy spending time with one another.

Family Words

Here are the Spanish words for family members.

grandfather	abuelo	(ah-BWAY-loh)
grandmother	abuela	(ah-BWAY-lah)
father	papi	(PAH-pee)
mother	mami	(MAH-mee)
uncle	tío	(TEE-oh)
aunt	tía	(TEE-ah)
son	hijo	(EE-hoh)
daughter	hija	(EE-hah)
brother	hermano	(her-MAH-noh)
sister	hermana	(her-MAH-nah)

Everyone helps cook, clean, and tend the garden. Children learn to respect older family members.

The people in a Puerto Rican family often work and play together.

23

Children take part in a festival for their town's patron saint.

Celebrate!

Most Puerto Ricans are Catholic. Many island celebrations are based on Catholic holidays. For example, every town in Puerto Rico has a Catholic patron saint. People believe that the saint looks out for the town. On special days, townspeople honor their saint with festivals.

Christmastime means presents for Puerto Rican children. But kids don't open gifts on Christmas Eve or Christmas Day. Instead, they get presents on the morning of Three Kings' Day. This holiday takes place on January 6.

Three Kings' Day is special for Puerto Rican Christians. It marks the day that three wise kings brought gifts to the baby Jesus.

Three boys dress up as kings to celebrate Three Kings' Day.

25

Spanish signs dot the streets in Puerto Rico. This sign says No Parking.

NO ESTACIONE

Strictly Speaking

Spanish is the language people speak in Puerto Rico. Many Puerto Ricans speak English as well.

Puerto Rican students study English in school. But islanders use Spanish to talk to one another.

A group of men plays dominoes on a street in Old San Juan. What language do you think they're speaking?

Old Buildings

Some Puerto Rican buildings are hundreds of years old.
Buildings with fancy balconies and windows line the streets.

These colorful buildings in San Juan have balconies facing the street.

El Morro

Pirates once sailed in Puerto Rico's waters. Islanders were afraid that the pirates would attack. Builders made a fortress to help protect San Juan. The fortress is called El Morro *(pictured at right).*

Builders finished El Morro in 1540. Its walls are nearly 20 feet (6 meters) thick. El Morro has tunnels and secret hiding places. But islanders were still afraid invaders would get in. In 1783, a giant wall was built. The wall wrapped around the whole city of San Juan! Pirates and invaders could not get past the wall.

The city of Ponce has a number of old buildings. The corners of some of these buildings are round.

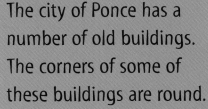

Ponce is a city in southern Puerto Rico. Puerto Ricans call Ponce the pearl of the south.

Puerto Ricans gobble up *tostones* when they want a snack.

Time to Eat

How would you like a plate of tostones? This snack is a favorite of many Puerto Ricans. Tostones are green plantains that have been fried. (Plantains are a type of starchy banana.)

For a hearty meal, try a bowl of *asopao*. That's a stew made with rice and meat or fish. Some popular desserts include mangoes and papaya. A custard called flan is another tasty treat.

Farmers in Puerto Rico grow fruits such as pineapples, bananas, mangoes, and papaya.

Off to School

To start out the school day right, most Puerto Rican kids eat breakfast. Scrambled eggs, sausage, or French toast may be served. Kids go off to school to study many subjects. They work hard to learn English, history, and math.

These school girls wear uniforms to their school in northwestern Puerto Rico.

Students also take classes in art and music. During recess, they sometimes jump rope or play games.

A man in costume gives a group of students a tour of historic buildings in San Juan.

Baseball Bonanza!

Baseball is big in Puerto Rico. Kids love to watch and play this game.

Puerto Rican boys play a game of baseball.

Fans pack the stadiums when their favorite teams are playing. Some Puerto Rican players have joined U.S. teams. Carlos Beltrán is one such player. He plays for the New York Mets.

Roberto Clemente

Roberto Clemente was a famous baseball star. He was born in Puerto Rico in 1934. Clemente was one of the best baseball players ever! He helped the Pittsburgh Pirates win two World Series. Clemente gave his time to many charities and causes. He died when he was only thirty-eight years old.

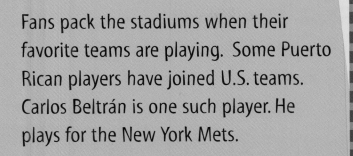

Roberto Clemente, shown here in 1955, is a baseball hero in Puerto Rico and the United States.

35

Feel the Beat

Salsa is the name for Puerto Rican dance music. Musicians blend African and Caribbean beats with jazz.

Puerto Ricans enjoy salsa music and dancing.

Salsa bands feature many singers and instruments. Some musicians shake maracas to keep time with the songs.

Dear Mom and Dad,

Puerto Rico rocks! Last night, Grandma and Grandpa took me to hear a salsa band. I could not sit still. Grandma has some salsa instruments at home. She showed me a maraca that rattles when you shake it. Guess what? It's made from a dried-out gourd! Seeds inside the gourd are what make the maraca rattle. Cha-cha-cha! Wish you were here!

Love,
Rita

Mom
You
Anyw

37

Bookworms

Education and literacy (the ability to read) are important in Puerto Rico. The island also has a rich tradition of storytelling.

Taino and African stories tell how the world came to be. Spanish settlers told tales about witches and princesses.

Literacy has an important place in Puerto Rican schools. The island has a very high literacy rate.

Some early Puerto Rican authors wrote about *jíbaros*. Jíbaros are peasant farmers. Modern writers may write about Puerto Rican culture. They may also tell stories of Puerto Ricans who have moved to the United States.

Juan Bobo

Juan Bobo (Simple John) is a jíbaro story character. He gets into funny situations. In one story, he dresses the family pig in his mother's best clothes. In another, he yells at a three-legged pot for being lazy. Juan thinks that a pot with three legs should be able to walk faster than he can.

Puerto Rican authors write about the country's culture. Music and dance are important parts of this culture.

Arts and Crafts

Mask making is popular in Puerto Rico. The most famous creations come from artists in the towns of Ponce and Loíza. People wear the masks at island festivals and parades.

Wearing masks at festivals is popular in Puerto Rico.

40

Other artists make wood carvings of saints. These religious statues are often brightly painted. Puerto Rican families keep them in their homes.

Wooden saints such as these are a common Puerto Rican craft item.

Vacation, Anyone?

Puerto Ricans enjoy relaxing at nearby parks after school and on weekends. City folks might spend free time visiting friends in the countryside.

This beach on the western coast of Puerto Rico is excellent for surfing.

Beaches are fun places for swimmers, surfers, and snorkelers. Others prefer to take long mountain hikes.

Paso Fino Fair

Horse lovers have fun at the Paso Fino Fair. This event takes place each March in the Puerto Rican town of Guayama. Riders compete on horseback in a series of events. They all ride *paso finos*. (That's a type of horse.)

Puerto Rico's beautiful parks are perfect spots for hiking.

THE FLAG OF PUERTO RICO

Puerto Rico's flag is red, white, and blue. It was designed to look like Cuba's flag. That's because both Puerto Rico and Cuba wanted to win freedom from Spain. The flag's white star stands for the Commonwealth of Puerto Rico.

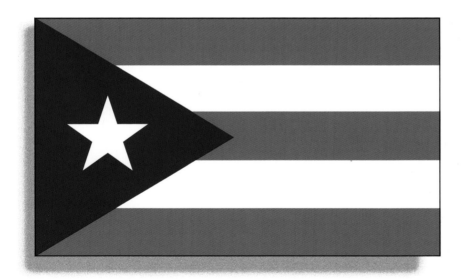

FAST FACTS

FULL COUNTRY NAME: Commonwealth of Puerto Rico

AREA: 3,435 square miles (8,897 square kilometers), or about the same size as Connecticut

MAIN LANDFORMS: the mountain ranges Cordillera Central, Luquillo, and Sierra de Cayey; the mountain peaks Cerro de Punta and El Yunque; the coastal lowlands; the coastal valleys

MAJOR RIVERS: Arecibo, La Plata, Culebrinas

ANIMALS AND THEIR HABITATS: Puerto Rican parrot, coquí (rain forest); lobsters, jellyfish, and blue parrot fish (ocean); leatherback turtles (Culebra Island); wild horses (Vieques Island); Mona iguanas (Mona Island)

CAPITAL CITY: San Juan

OFFICIAL LANGUAGES: Spanish and English

POPULATION: about 3,958,128

GLOSSARY

cove: a small, shallow inlet

crater: a hole in the ground shaped like a bowl

culture: the way of life, ideas, and customs of a particular group of people

hurricane: a big storm with strong winds and heavy rain

island: a piece of land surrounded by water

karst: an irregular landscape made up of a soft rock called limestone. Karst regions contain hills, caves, craters, and underground streams.

map: a drawing or chart of all or part of Earth or the sky

mountain: a part of Earth's surface that rises high into the sky

plantation: a large farm. Spanish settlers forced Puerto Rico's native people to work on plantations.

rain forest: a thick, green forest that gets lots of rain

salsa: a type of Puerto Rican dance music

tropical: warm and rainy

U.S. commonwealth: a territory that is owned by the United States

valley: a low-lying piece of land

TO LEARN MORE

BOOKS

Bernier-Grand, Carmen T. *Shake It, Morena!: And Other Folklore from Puerto Rico.* Minneapolis: Millbrook Press, 2002. Puerto Rican games, songs, and riddles come to life in this brightly illustrated selection.

Heinrichs, Ann. *Puerto Rico.* Mankato, MN: Child's World, 2006. Learn more about the history and people of Puerto Rico in this interesting book.

Johnston, Joyce. *Puerto Rico.* Minneapolis: Lerner Publications Company, 2002. This title takes a detailed and in-depth look at Puerto Rico.

Montes, Marisa. *Juan Bobo Goes to Work.* New York: HarperCollins Publishers, 2000. Read a fun and funny tale about Juan Bobo, a well-known Puerto Rican story character.

WEBSITES

Enchanted Learning
http://www.enchantedlearning.com/geography
This site has pages to label and color of Puerto Rico and its flag.

Puerto Rico
http://www.timeforkids.com/TFK/kids/hh/goplaces/main/0,28375,702661,00.html
On this fun site from *Time for Kids*, you can take a virtual tour of Puerto Rico, learn some Taino words and phrases, and send a postcard to a friend.

INDEX